Mountains in their rugged grandeur have always presented a challenge to man. *All About Mountains and Mountaineering* is the story of the world's great ranges and of the men who met their challenge.

Where did the mountains come from? Are they all the same age? How were the different kinds of mountains formed? In this book, you will read of block mountains, folded mountains, and volcanic mountains—of islands that are the tops of volcanoes and others that are peaks of the mighty Atlantic Ridge.

Here are the Alps, with their avalanches and glaciers and blinding snows; the fur-rich Rockies, standing as a barrier to Americans; the treasure-filled Andes, which the Indians conquered; and the Himalayas, top of the world, most challenging of all mountains.

With unusual narrative skill, Anne Terry White tells the stirring tale of men against mountains, and presents the drama and suspense of great achievements in mountaineering.

ALL ABOUT
MOUNTAINS
AND MOUNTAINEERING

ALL ABOUT

THIS SPECIAL EDITION IS PRINTED AND DISTRIBUTED BY
ARRANGEMENT WITH THE ORIGINATORS AND PUBLISHERS
OF ALL ABOUT BOOKS *Random House, Inc.,* NEW YORK, BY

E. M. HALE AND COMPANY
EAU CLAIRE, WISCONSIN

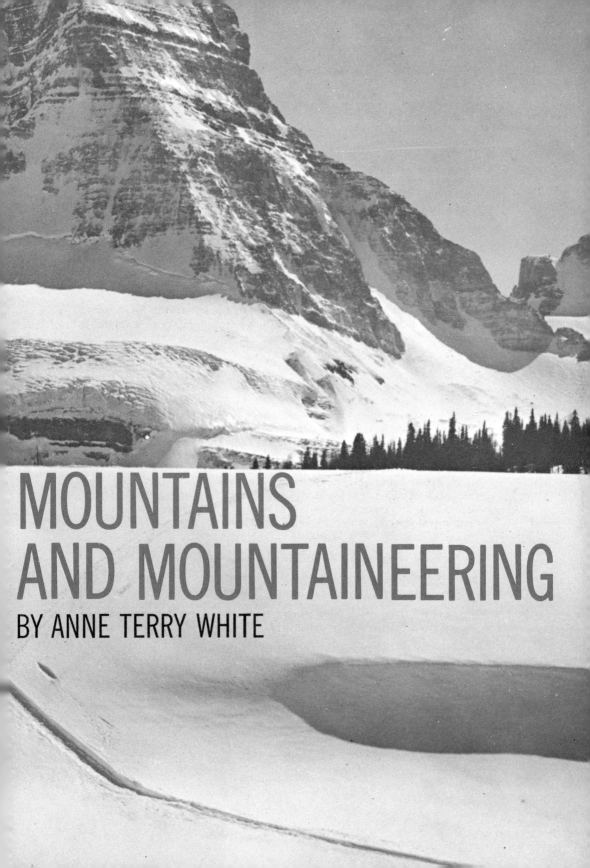

MOUNTAINS AND MOUNTAINEERING

BY ANNE TERRY WHITE

By special permission of G. P. Putnam's Sons, parts of the two final chapters of this book are adapted from *Tiger of the Snows,* the autobiography of Tenzing of Everest, written in collaboration with James Ramsey Ullman. Copyright © 1955 by Tenzing Norgay and James Ramsey Ullman.

Grateful acknowledgment is also due to George G. Harrap & Company, Limited, which first published Tenzing's autobiography in England as *Man of Everest.*

PHOTOGRAPH CREDITS: Ansel Adams (*Magnum*), pages 59, 65; Alpine Museum, Zermatt, Switzerland, 44; Dr. George Bell, 84, 87, 106–107, 123, 137; Canadian National Railways, endpaper, 60; Canadian Pacific Railway, ii–iii, 12; Georgia Engelhard (*Monkmeyer*), 49, 50, 54, 55, 69; Fairchild Aerial Surveys, 98, 102; French Government Tourist Office, 35, 40; Ewing Galloway, 5; J. B. Guss (*Black Star*), 85; George Holton, 89; Sergio Larrain (*Magnum*), 91; Monkmeyer Press Photo Service, 39, 70, 114, 116, 117, 120; Josef Muench, cover; Vittorio Sella (*Ewing Galloway*), 109; Silberstein (*Monkmeyer*), 96; Standard Oil Company (N. J.), 61, 66; Marga Steinmann, St. Gall (*Swiss National Tourist Office*), 26; Swiss National Tourist Office, 7, 31; S. A. Tourist (*Monkmeyer*), 11; United Press International, 130–131, 135, 136; U. S. Navy, 13; Bradford Washburn, 19, 24, 73, 78, 80; Bradford Washburn (*Fairchild Aerial Surveys*), 77; Wide World, 15, 124.

For helpful suggestions about this book, grateful acknowledgment is made to Gerard L. Alexander, Chief, Map Division, New York Public Library; Charles L. Drake, Lamont Geological Observatory, Columbia University; J. P. Duminy, Principal, University of Cape Town, South Africa; Bradford Washburn, Director, Museum of Science, Boston; and Walter A. Wood, President, American Geographical Society, New York.

DESIGN BY ROBERT KORN

To Tenzing of Everest

AUTHOR'S NOTE

I wish to acknowledge my debt to James Ramsey Ullman, whose Age of Mountaineering *is an excellent book on the subject. I also wish to recommend Tenzing Norgay's autobiography,* Tiger of the Snows, *written by Tenzing in collaboration with Ullman. It is a moving and stirring book.*

CONTENTS

5. The Himalayas

ALL ABOUT
MOUNTAINS
AND MOUNTAINEERING

1 The Earth's High Places

There the mountains are

Running down the length of the Americas, from Alaska to Cape Horn, is a vast chain of high mountains. The Rockies we call them in North America, the Andes in South America. It would be hard to think of the New World without that rugged backbone.

Yet it was not always there. The Rockies and the Andes are quite new. It is only some sixty million years since the Rockies began to rise out of the sea. The Andes are newer still. They are among the newest of the earth's mountains and, indeed, are still rising.

What about the other great ranges of the world?

3

We could say the same thing about them. The Himalayas are so young that, like the Andes, they are still going up. Other ranges are somewhat older, but none of the earth's mountains are really old. The old mountains are nearly gone.

Gone where?

They have been worn away. Rain and sun, snow and frost and wind and the air itself have weathered the mountains away. Rivers have sawed their way through them. Glaciers have plowed over them. The rocks broke into chunks, the chunks into chips. The chips wore down into pebbles, the pebbles into sand and silt. Grain by grain the streams carried the mountains into the sea. Only their gnarled and twisted roots are left to show that once those mountains were there.

Man is lucky. Through most of the earth's long story, the continents have been much lower than they are now. Seas have rolled over them time and again. Once a shallow sea a thousand miles wide flowed where the Rockies tower. A quarter of all North America was under water then. Seas rolled where the Cascades and the Andes rise. A monster sea, stretching from Gibraltar to southeast Asia, flowed where the Alps, the Caucasus, and the Himalayas stand. The Mediterranean, the Black Sea, and the Caspian are all remnants of that one great sea.

Man is lucky. He lives in an age of high continents crowned by lofty mountains. His stage is beautifully set. He lifts up his eyes and there the mountains are. . . .

There the mountains are—and from the very beginning man has risen to their challenge.

"What lies beyond?" he asked—and did not rest till he found out. Sometimes he went around the mountains. Sometimes he forged his way through, discovering the passes. Sometimes the mountains held him up, and he stayed and settled there and overcame the hard conditions of his life. Four thousand years ago, Stone Age farmers built villages on stilts high in the Alps by the

Japan's Fujiyama, one of the world's most beautiful mountains.

lakes of Switzerland. Perhaps as long as two thousand years ago, Indians took over the high Andes in Peru and built terraced farms upon the barren slopes.

"What treasure do the mountains hold?" man asked. He explored the high forests and the streams. He hunted, trapped, fished, and lumbered. He learned the virtues of the mountain plants and bred them to his uses. He bred the llama from the wild guanaco. He tamed the yak and the two-humped camel. He found the gold, the copper, silver, platinum, tin. He took the emeralds, crystals, and other gems. He found the coal.

"There is safety on the heights," man said—and fled to the sheer rock to preserve his freedom. For lowlands are easy to overrun, but mountains are hideouts where one man is equal to a thousand.

Last of all man met the challenge of the peaks. "I will set my feet where no one has ever stood before," man said. He braved the snow and ice, the avalanche and rockfall, the precipice and crevasse, the freezing cold and scarcity of oxygen. He climbed the Alps, he climbed the Caucasus. He climbed the Rockies, the Andes, and the Himalayas. He kept on climbing until he stood on the very top of the earth.

Toiling up a long ridge.

The coming of the mountains

How many mountains are there?

No one has counted the individual peaks. But we can say that roughly a fourth of the land area of the earth is mountainous. One of the mountainous areas runs right around the Pacific. Another crosses Europe and Asia, from Gibraltar to the Pacific again. The Atlas Mountains in northwest Africa are part of that high band. Once they were thought to be the highest mountains of all. The Greeks, who had a story about everything, set their Titan Atlas there to hold the world up on his shoulders.

8

There are great differences in the heights of mountains. The Himalayas are towering giants. The Urals, on the other hand, those mineral-rich mountains which seem to divide Europe from Asia, are so worn down that many of them are no more than a thousand feet high. Their highest peak is only 5,540 feet.

Still, we call them *mountains*, while we call some higher mountains *hills*.

When is a hill not a hill?

There isn't any rule. In western South Dakota, we call the mountains Black Hills though one of their peaks is a thousand feet higher than New Hampshire's Mount Washington. There isn't any rule, and yet—

Does your land mass stand out conspicuously? Then you have a right to call it a mountain. On the other hand, even a quite high mountain may be called a foothill if it stands near mountains that are much higher.

Are mountains all alike except for size?

Naturally, size is the first thing that strikes us about a mountain. But size doesn't tell us much. Two mountains may be the same size and yet their stories may be totally different. For mountains have come into the world not only at different times but also in different ways. Some mountains have been simply pushed up. Others have been folded into wrinkles. And some have been built out of stuff that came pouring from the hot interior of the earth.

How wonderful it would be if we could look inside this planet of ours and see the mountain-making forces doing their work! Of course, we would have to telescope time so that centuries became moments, for mountain building is a slow process. We would see rock responding to pressure. We would see the rock bend the way steel bends when slowly, slowly great pressure is applied. The rock would bend, and suddenly—when it could stand no more strain—it would snap. Then up on the surface people would feel the vibration set up by that monstrous snap. "Earthquake!" they would cry and grow pale, for it is terrifying to have the solid earth shake under your feet.

Perhaps the rock would break all the way to the top of the earth and people would see the rift. Perhaps one broken end would rise right up above the earth. Perhaps over the years that broken end would be pushed up and up till it became a great, high mountain. We would call it a *block* mountain.

We have mountains like that in the United States. The Sierra Nevada are mountains of this kind. That whole great range—400 miles long and 60 miles wide— is just one enormous tilted block of rock that snapped and moved up. The block is steep on one side and

Above South Africa's Table Mountain, there is often a white cloud. People call it the Tablecloth.

gently sloping on the other. The side facing the east is where the rock broke and was pushed up. It rises on that side more than two miles above the desert. The side facing the Pacific is the sloping top of the block.

The Tetons are another range of block mountains.

Sometimes, as we looked down into the earth, we would see rock under great pressure break not in just one place but all around. Then we would see the entire broken block pushed up like a table. The Ruwenzori mountains of central Africa are like that.

Mount Assiniboine in the Canadian Rockies.

There are many block mountains in the world, but the greatest ranges were made in a different way. The Alps, the Caucasus, the Appalachians, the Rockies, the Andes, the Himalayas, and other great ranges are all *folded* mountains—wrinkle ranges.

Scientists used to believe that those great wrinkles on the face of the earth were made when the hot earth cooled and shrank. "It's like a baked apple," they thought. "When the apple cools, it shrinks. The skin gets too big and has to fold into wrinkles around the core."

We know now that the great ranges were not made that way. Those folds are not the result of cooling. The

Italy's Mount Vesuvius. In 79 A.D. *two cities, Pompeii and Herculaneum, were buried when this volcano erupted after a sleep of a thousand years.*

great ranges were wrinkled the way a tablecloth is wrinkled when you hold it down with one hand and push with the other. Or when you hold it down with both hands and slide the hands towards each other. Scientists don't all agree as to what caused the pushing. But all are of the same opinion about this: the great ranges rose out of shallow seas. They are all pushed-up, wrinkled sea floors. The sea shells found high on the mountainsides are proof of that.

It takes a very long time for nature to make mountains out of the floor of a sea. Perhaps it takes even longer than to make a block mountain. But another kind of mountain grows fast—a volcano. A *volcanic* mountain may build up so fast that we don't even have to telescope time to watch it grow. After a new volcano was born in a Mexican cornfield in 1943, we learned that in just nine years a volcano can build a cone 1,600 feet high.

A volcano is one of nature's mysteries, for no one is quite sure what makes the rock come boiling up out of the earth. Perhaps radioactive elements cause the rock to melt in some little pocket deep down. Anyway the boiling rock comes up. At a weak place in the earth's crust, it breaks through. Out come the pent-up steam and gases that have formed in the molten rock. And with them come red-hot rocks. The "cinders" shoot up and fall down again around the opening, building up a cone. Later on, molten stone—lava—generally comes pouring out. It pours down the sides of the cone and builds it bigger and bigger till a great mountain is formed.

In the United States we have every kind of mountain, including volcanic mountains—active, sleeping, and dead. And since Hawaii became a state, we can boast of having the greatest of all shield volcanoes. For that is what the Hawaiian Islands are—the tops of volcanoes.

Shield volcanoes are not cone-shaped. The reason is that the molten stone pouring out of them has very little gas in it. So instead of bursting out violently and coming down in one spot, the lava just flows gently away. Naturally, it takes much longer to build up a shield than a cone. But slowly, slowly over the years the mountaintop gets higher and higher. Finally it gets so high that it rises above the ocean, and men see a new island.

Eye witnesses say that few events are more exciting than the birth of an island. The water of the ocean seems to boil and bubble. Steam pours forth. Volcanic ash and pumice come floating up from the depths together with dead fish and other creatures of the sea.

Boiling lava from Hawaii's Mauna Loa pours down a cliffside into the sea. The stream is 50 feet wide.

The newborn island is the summit of a high mountain that has been silently building up over the years and now at last comes up into the light and air.

Nearly all the islands of the deep sea far from the continents are shield volcanoes. But not all. A few are the peaks of a vast volcanic mountain range.

Until a hundred years ago no one suspected there was a range of mountains under the sea. Then a route was surveyed for a transatlantic cable—and the range was discovered. The Atlantic Ridge, as the undersea mountains were named, is the earth's longest mountain chain. The Ridge is thousands of miles long—longer than the Rockies and the Andes put together. It curves in a sort of letter S through the North and South Atlantic till it is just opposite Cape Horn. There it takes a sharp turn east and runs on toward the Indian and Pacific Oceans.

The Atlantic Ridge is twice as wide as the Andes and several times as wide as the Appalachians. Its central backbone is a mile or two above the floor of the sea, and there is a mile of water above the crest of the Ridge. But its high peaks reach up through the waves to the light of day. It is some peaks of the Atlantic Ridge that are known as the Rocks of St. Paul. There they are near the equator in the mid-Atlantic, half a dozen little specks not more than half a mile across in all. They were a mystery once. Now

that we know the Atlantic Ridge is there, we understand them.

We understand Ascension Island, Tristan da Cunha,
Gough and Bouvet, too, for all these are peaks of the
Atlantic Ridge. And so is Pico Island in the Azores.
Pico Island is the highest peak of the Atlantic Ridge.
From the floor of the ocean it rises 27,000 feet. That
is over five miles. Not many of the earth's mountains
are higher than this peak that soars up from the bottom
of the sea.

Rivers of ice

Perhaps the most striking parts of the world's great mountains are the rivers of ice called glaciers. In the high valleys of the Alps there are 1,200 of them, the biggest being 13½ miles long. In other high mountains there are many much bigger ones. The Hubbard Glacier, winding for 72 miles through parts of Canada and Alaska, contains more snow and ice than all the glaciers in Switzerland put together. Alaska's Malaspina Glacier is larger still. It is almost as big as Rhode Island.

From a distance a glacier doesn't look as if it is made of ice. It looks rather like a streak of snow, and

Great rivers of ice flow together to form Alaska's Barnard Glacier.

even a few steps away you have a hard time persuading yourself that this is really ice. For it isn't glittering and polished like the ice we skate on, but rough and uneven. And the reason for the difference is this: The ice of glaciers is made not of water but of snow. Its surface often becomes matted and pockmarked by fierce winds. What is more, as a glacier moves, pressure keeps roughening and changing its top. Frequently the ice is broken up in towers, called *seracs*, some of which are high as church steeples. As the ice passes over uneven ground, crevasses open and close in it. There may be a whole network of these huge cracks, often with snow bridges over them.

A river of ice will form where year after year more snow falls than melts away. The snowflakes lose their points. They turn into little grains of ice, something like grains of sand. These are pressed together until they become solid ice.

A glacier does not stand still. Gravity keeps pulling it down and the mass above pushes it down. But how fast it travels depends on a lot of things. How big is the glacier? How steep is the slope? How cold is the weather? On sunny days a glacier may move twice as fast as on cloudy days. In Greenland, with the great icecap pushing behind, some glaciers move fifty or sixty feet a day. Even speedy Swiss glaciers move only a few feet a day.

Naturally, the closer a mountain is to the North or
South Pole, the more likely it is to have glaciers—
provided there is snow. But even near the equator a
high mountain is apt to have one or more rivers of
ice. For temperature is a question not only of latitude
but also of height. The higher up you go, the colder
it gets. Mount Kilimanjaro in Africa is close to the
equator, yet it has three great glaciers.

2 The Alps

Snow on the mountains

The Alps are deeply folded mountains. Here the land has been folded so much to make these mountains that Switzerland would be 150 miles wider if they weren't there. But the Alps extend far beyond Switzerland. There are French Alps and Italian Alps, Austrian and German Alps.

These are cheerful heights, mountains that lift the heart not only by their beauty. There is so much sparkling fresh water here! In the Alps there is water enough for half of Europe. There is water enough for four great rivers to be born—the Rhone and the Rhine,

the Po and the Danube. Millions of tons of water flow from the melting glaciers. On an average, thirty-three feet of snow fall every year.

That is a lot of snow. But from very early times men learned to live with it, for even the smallest piece of land that can be farmed is precious in Europe. Stone Age man pastured his sheep on these very same *alps*, as the mountain pastures are called, and sowed his little fields of barley in the same high valleys. Modern man has even managed to turn the heavy snow to his advantage. For good snow attracts tourists and turns the Alps into the playground of Europe.

But snow in the mountains also brings the terror of the avalanche—the danger of masses of snow rushing down the slopes.

Avalanches are not peculiar to the Alps. In the other great ranges, however, the rushing snow spells danger mainly to mountain climbers, for those mountains are not thickly settled. In the Alps avalanches are a terror to houses and farms and even to whole villages.

In the early spring, when snow turns wet and heavy and seeping water loosens the under layer, thousands of snow cataracts rush down. Wet-snow avalanches occur so regularly in the same place that you can see where they have furrowed the rock. They run like rivers in their channels. Mountaineers who know the

Beside the Swiss Alps, a man-made dam appears insignificant.

An avalanche roars down the Jungfrau.

dangerous avalanche tracks cross them in a hurry—without speaking a word. They know that even the vibrations of a human voice may start a mass of snow that is just balancing on a slope.

Dangerous as these spring avalanches are, the "dry" snow cataracts that come in dead of winter are worse. They are the most dreaded of all avalanches because fierce whirlwinds come with them. The snow shoots down the slope so fast that it drives a column of compressed air before it. Behind and at the sides a vacuum is left that sucks in nearby objects.

Such avalanches are most likely to start at a time when new snow has fallen and has not yet stuck to the hardened snow beneath. Then the tread of a chamois is enough to disturb the upper sheet of snow. The fall of a branch is enough. The sound of a passing plane or even an echo is enough to do it. At first the top snow slides slowly over the hardened mass beneath. Then it rushes down. Other beds of snow join in. Stones, brushwood, earth hurry along with it. The avalanche tears down trees. It sweeps away houses in its path. And like the side of a mountain that gives way, it plunges into the valley. Sometimes the rush is so great that the mass thunders across the valley floor and piles up against the opposite slope.

Over the centuries countless lives have been lost in avalanches. One of the blackest years was 1951. In Switzerland alone 234 people were caught in avalanches and 98 of them killed.

The people of the Alps fight back. They plant trees on the heights. They put up barricades in steep side valleys to hold back the rushing snow. And when they see a mass starting to pile up on some ledge, they don't wait for it to fall. As though it were a living enemy, they attack it with mortar fire. They force the snow to fall before it becomes a danger.

Crossing the Alps

The Alps have a great many passes. For after the mountains were folded lengthwise, they were squeezed the other way, making low places across the chains. Some of these passes lead from valley to valley. Others go all the way across.

To the Romans, in their early days, the Alps were the "walls of Rome." Stretching like a bow across the top of Italy, the Alps seemed like ramparts that would keep the enemy out. The Romans were so sure of their "walls" that they never thought to guard the passes.

In the year 218 B.C., they had an unpleasant surprise. At that time they were carrying on a fight-to-the-death with the Carthaginians, just across the Mediterranean. The Romans had destroyed the enemy's navy. But the Carthaginians weren't crushed. Hannibal, their young general, made up his mind to destroy Rome before Rome destroyed Carthage.

How could he get his troops to Italy now that Carthage had lost her navy?

Hannibal decided to march overland from Spain. He would go over the Pyrenees, cross southern France, and pass over the Alps into Italy. It would be a journey of 1,500 miles. Hardest of all would be getting his trained war elephants over the mountains. Yet he must have them, for they were his surprise weapon. The sight of the huge beasts, the smell of them, and the noise of their wild trumpeting terrified both men and horses. When the elephants charged, fighting with tusk and trunk and trampling with their big feet, no enemy could stand against them.

It took Hannibal five months to get to the Alps with his 40,000 men, his horses, and his elephants. But the worst was still ahead. When his men looked up at those awful heights, their hearts sank.

The climb began. No sooner had the Carthaginians entered the gorges, however, than the wild tribes of the Alps began to attack from above. Some hurled spears, some rolled down boulders. On one side was a sheer drop, on the other a cliff impossible to scale. The wounded horses turned back on the pack animals, many of which fell to the bottom together with their loads. Others bolted forward, brushing aside everything in their way. Only when the elephants led the column did the enemy give Hannibal peace. Then they didn't dare to attack for fear of the strange beasts.

Many a time the army took the wrong turning. Many a time they had to retrace their steps. Sometimes their Gallic guides led them astray on purpose. Sometimes the troops, trying to find their own way, got lost in the mountain mazes. On the ninth day in the Alps, Hannibal reached the top of the pass. From here the Carthaginian looked down into Italy. Behind him and on either hand the Alps rose peak behind peak, like row upon row of battlements. He stretched out his arm and pointed in the direction of Rome. "There lies the enemy of Carthage!" he cried.

Late on the fifteenth day the general led his troops into the valley of the Po. He had lost 18,000 foot soldiers and 2,000 horses—half his forces. But he had crossed the Alps. He was in Italy. He was behind Rome.

Nearly twenty-two centuries have passed since Hannibal made that crossing, and the wonder of it is with us still. For it was the most daring mountain crossing of all time. And it was the first.

Later, Julius Caesar led his legions north across the Alps to conquer Gaul. The Goths and Huns came back the other way to lay waste Rome and Italy. Charlemagne led his troops across. Napoleon came with 40,000 men. They dragged their cannon to the Great St. Bernard Pass in hollowed-out tree trunks through slush up to their knees, a hundred men pulling on a log.

It was a remarkable feat, for this pass is 8,200 feet high. At the top the temperature seldom gets above 50° Fahrenheit. This is a region of wind and sleet and snow.

Here stands the Hospice of St. Bernard. In years gone by the monks of the Hospice and their noble St. Bernard dogs rescued many travelers from icy death. One famous

St. Bernard dogs were trained for rescue work by the monks of the Hospice.

dog named Barry saved forty-one lives.

A thousand years have gone by since the Hospice of St. Bernard was opened. Hundreds and hundreds of people have been saved from death in that time. Thousands upon thousands have been fed and lodged and cared for there. At one time 20,000 people a year crossed the pass. Not one was ever turned away or was asked to pay for what he received.

Nowadays there are a railway and a tunnel. The merchants with rich goods from the East, the pilgrims going to the Holy Land, are gone. Those who go over the pass and stop at the Hospice today are mainly workers too poor to pay railway fare. Sometimes an army deserter comes through—sometimes a smuggler. The good brothers ask no questions. They give the same welcome and the same food to all.

The birth of mountaineering

Once someone asked George Leigh Mallory, a famous British mountaineer who later lost his life on Mount Everest: "Why do you want to climb this mountain?"

Mallory answered: "Because it is there."

We can understand how he felt. He wanted to test himself, to pit his strength against the mountain's difficulties, to conquer it by standing on its highest peak. But this feeling of ours is something modern. In earlier days, nobody thought of climbing mountains, for they were places of fear. They were a sort of no-man's land between earth and heaven. The Greeks said the gods lived on Mount Olympus, but they didn't climb up to see.

Until about two hundred years ago nobody climbed mountains at all. A few men sometimes risked their lives in the Alps to hunt chamois or pick crystals from the rocks to sell for a few francs. But they didn't climb high. And the idea of standing on top of snowy Mont Blanc, giant of the Alps, never crossed anybody's mind.

Mont Blanc—15,782 feet—is the highest peak in the Alps. It lies about fifty miles from Geneva, with its broad base resting partly in France and partly in Italy. This is where the first great climbs were made. In this region the modern method of rock-climbing was born. And here almost every European climber learned his mountaineering ABC's.

Horace Benedict de Saussure was the father of it all.

He was a young scholar and gentleman of wealth who came to Chamonix in 1760 to see beautiful Mont Blanc. He had always had a passion for mountains, and now he was making a collection of alpine plants. He told himself that his interest in Mont Blanc was purely scientific. But as he looked at the peak, a strange new feeling took hold of him: he wanted to stand on its top. He hired a chamois-hunter to take him up to the Mer de Glace, the "Sea of Ice" flowing off the flank of Mont Blanc.

The "Mer de Glace" glacier on Mont Blanc looks like a choppy sea.

The glacier looked like its name—a sea frozen in a storm. Its surface was covered with ice ridges like waves. Deep, dangerous crevasses had opened up in it.

Afterward De Saussure studied the ice and snow of the mountainside through a telescope. In imagination he picked his way through piles of fallen ice and struggled up the rocky ridges that led to the great white dome. The top could be reached and it should! Before leaving, he went to every village near by and posted a notice offering a reward to the first man who reached the summit.

Many years passed, yet no one claimed the reward. But meantime Horace de Saussure had become a noted scientist, and the fact that he talked so much about climbing Mont Blanc brought tourists to Chamonix. A few of them hired hunters to take them up as high as they dared.

Some of the most daring came down looking exceedingly pale. There really *was* something to be afraid of on the heights. Their hearts had started to beat fast and their breath came short. Some of the climbers had even become dizzy and nauseated, while others got splitting headaches. Had they caught a strange mountain sickness?

Nobody as yet understood that the higher you go, the less oxygen there is. Years were to pass before people stopped worrying about the pounding of their hearts.

Dr. Paccard of Chamonix was one of the most persistent of the climbers. By 1786 this mountaineer had tried and failed to get to the top by several different routes. That summer he decided to try one that had never been attempted before—directly by the side which faces Chamonix—right up the middle! No guide had tried to go that way, because they doubted that a climber could get to the top and be back before night. And nobody had the courage to stay all night on the snow. For it was supposed that you could not live through such an ordeal. However, Dr. Paccard knew that a young hunter of chamois and crystals, Jacques Balmat by name, had recently been caught by darkness on the mountain. He had spent the night in a snowstorm at 14,000 feet.

Now the doctor didn't have much money and couldn't afford to pay a guide. So he was planning to go up alone, dangerous though that was. But Balmat came to him. "Let me go with you," he begged. "Pay me as a porter if you can't afford a guide." Balmat was willing to take a porter's small fee because he dreamed of winning De Saussure's prize.

On the morning of August 7, the two men set out. Their heavy packs held a blanket, food for several days, and instruments. In his right hand each had an alpenstock. The strong staff was good to lean on, while the metal point could be used to chip steps in the ice.

The conditions for climbing were so bad that the adventure almost ended on the glacier. For it had rained for a week before they started.

The two men were relieved when at last they got to a long, rocky ridge that reaches high up onto the slopes of Mont Blanc, where it lies like a narrow island between two glaciers. Here they made good time. But when they got farther up, where the glaciers join, they again found themselves in a mess of ice. Night was coming on. So they ate, rolled up in their one blanket under an overhanging rock, and went to sleep. They were still only about a mile and a half above sea level and had two more upward miles to go.

At 4:00 A.M. they were up and off along the ice. Things were much worse than the day before. Again and again they had to cross crevasses whose snow bridges couldn't be trusted. Often they were forced to make bridges of their own. They would follow a cre- vasse to a narrow point, put their two alpenstocks side by side across it, and slide over the crevasse on them.

About 3:00 P.M. they finished struggling up the steep slope of a great snowfield under the dome. Another snowfield lay above. Balmat took a few steps on it, saw that the crust wouldn't hold him, and stopped.

For a moment he stared up at the tilted whiteness, then turned back. "I am not going any farther," he said. He had broken trail nearly all the way and had carried the heavier load. Now he was too tired to plod through soft snow.

Paccard begged him to go on, but Balmat shook his head. "It is too late," he said wearily.

"But we are almost there," the doctor pleaded. "It can't be more than three thousand feet to the summit. Come! I will carry more of the load. I will take turns with you in breaking trail."

At last Balmat agreed. He followed the doctor across

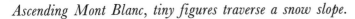

Ascending Mont Blanc, tiny figures traverse a snow slope.

Mountaineers plod up Mont Blanc. To prevent slipping, they wear crampons strapped to their boots.

the snowfield toward two ridges of red rock. Here, to their relief, the two men found that the wind had blown the top snow away, leaving bare the glazed crust to the right of the two ridges. They took turns chipping footholds in the ice crust with their alpenstocks.

Step by slow step they went up. Two hours passed before they reached the top of the red rocks. Now only the gentle slope to the summit lay ahead. They struggled on, bent double under the icy wind, taking turns leading. At first they were able to take a hundred steps before they needed to stop and rest. Then it was eighty. Then fifty. At last they were stopping every fourteen steps. The doctor was leading when, straightening up for a moment, he made out an edge of blue above the dome. It was the sky! With a shout he hurried on. Balmat broke into a run to catch up with him. And they stood on the summit of Mont Blanc.

Breathlessly they looked around at the view which no human being had ever seen before. Then with his frost-bitten hands Dr. Paccard took the temperature.

Dusk was gathering and they started down. They had no idea that their victory was already known below, that a telescope had been trained on them for the last hour and a half, and that every step of the final climb had been eagerly followed. The church bells in Chamonix were ringing wildly.

To the top of the Matterhorn

A year after Paccard and Balmat had reached the top of Mont Blanc, De Saussure himself stood on the summit. And after that climbers went up and down endlessly.

They copied De Saussure in every particular. He had gone up wearing spiked crampons strapped to his boots to get a better grip on snow and ice. So all the climbers wore spiked crampons strapped to their boots. They put on black crepe masks to protect their faces from sunburn just as he had done. Like him they carried food, a tent, ropes, ladders to bridge crevasses, and ice axes to cut steps. And they also carried scientific instruments. For no one would as yet admit that he was climbing just for the joy of it.

For fifty years mountaineering was nothing but climbing Mont Blanc. It was as though no other mountains existed. But finally bold spirits began to dare other peaks. And by the 1860's, out of hundreds of Alpine peaks only a handful remained unconquered.

The Matterhorn was one.

The Matterhorn rises like a monument on the border between Switzerland and Italy. Many of its snowy neighbor peaks are nearly as high, while several are even higher. But the eye comes to rest on that almost bare, soaring rock that rises in a pyramid nearly a mile above its glaciers. The cliffs of the Matterhorn are steep and sheer. Very little snow can stay on them and there is nothing to protect the rock from the sun. By day the cliffs expand. At night they contract with the cold. There is a constant cracking and loosening and sliding of rock in deadly avalanches. To the eye, the Matterhorn presents a mountain of terrible danger.

Year after year, experienced mountaineers tried to climb it. They failed. Many decided it was an unconquerable peak.

In 1865 Edward Whymper, artist and illustrator, conquered the unconquerable Matterhorn.

Whymper first came to Switzerland in the summer of 1860. The handsome young man of twenty came planning to sketch for a few weeks. He meant to climb only high enough to find good views to sketch. But he was no sooner in the Alps than he became a mountaineer. Then he saw the Matterhorn and fell in love with it, as many others have done before and since.

In the years that followed, Whymper tried six times to reach the top. Each time he was beaten back. In 1865 he came back to the Italian village of Breuil for another try.

All the attempts to climb the Matterhorn had been made by the southwest ridge because the northeast side of the mountain looked so steep. But Whymper had noticed that patches of snow remained on the east face all through the summer. How could that be? Loose snow would not stay permanently on rock that sloped much more than 45 degrees. Probably the east face was not so steep as it looked. In that case, the ridge beside it might not be as steep as it looked either.

He determined to try the mountain from the northeast. With four guides he started up. But a rock fall that almost killed them took the heart out of the party, and the seventh attempt failed too. His guides refused to go up with him again.

Whymper was not dismayed. He knew that the best

Edward Whymper at the age of 25, shortly before his successful ascent of the Matterhorn.

guide in Europe, an Italian Swiss named Jean-Antoine Carrel, wanted to attempt the Matterhorn. Like Whymper, Carrel believed that the great peak could be climbed.

"I will try the east face with you," Carrel agreed at once when the Englishman approached him.

They waited for good weather. But when it came, the day brought sharp disappointment to Whymper. A party of Italians were in Breuil. They were going to climb the mountain by the southwest ridge. Carrel—who wanted the glory of reaching the summit to go to the Italians—had joined their party.

Taken aback, Whymper tried to hire some other guide. But not a guide or porter was to be had—the Italians had taken them all.

Just then a young English climber, Lord Francis Douglas, arrived in Breuil with his porter, Peter Taugwalder. They had come from Zermatt across the pass.

"I'd like to try the Matterhorn," Douglas said when he heard Whymper's story. "Peter's father has heard of your plan. He agrees that the mountain can be climbed by the east face. Probably he would like to join us."

The three hurried to Zermatt and made sure that Peter Taugwalder's father, who was a noted guide, would come too. And that night three others joined the party. They were Charles Hudson, a clergyman, who was considered the best amateur climber of the day;

his 19-year-old companion Hadow; and their guide, Michel Croz. They made plans to start at 5:30 next morning.

The first day's climb was easy. The seven mountaineers were full of good spirits as they made camp at 11,000 feet. They laughed and sang till long after dusk and at the first light of day were on the way again. Above them the east face towered nearly 4,000 feet. But, as Whymper had guessed, this side of the mountain was not so steep as it looked. Here, because the layers of rock were tilted upward, the mountainside rose in a great natural staircase, and all except Hadow climbed it easily. Hadow's boots were giving him trouble—the nails on them were worn smooth and he slipped constantly.

By 10:00 A.M. the climbers were at 14,000 feet. They had only a few more hundred upward feet to go. But from this point the east face was an almost upright wall, impossible to climb. For a little while they followed the crest of the northeast ridge. Then they saw they would have to cross over to the north face and creep up the edge of that instead.

So they crossed. To their dismay they found the north face covered with a thin layer of ice. It would take all their mountaineering skill to climb it. With one slip, a man might fall all the way to the Matterhorn glacier, 4,000 feet below. They roped up for safety and moved forward one by one.

For about 400 feet they made their way thus across the north face. Then they went straight up for 60 feet and cut back to the crest of the northeast ridge. Here they met another difficulty. At the very top of the ridge a rock protruded. They had somehow to get around it. Advancing with the greatest care, they made it. When they looked up, their hearts began to pound with joy, for now only an easy snow slope was above them.

Whymper and Croz got to the top together.

Were they the first to arrive?

Whymper looked anxiously for footprints in the snow. To his relief he could see none but their own. Then he looked down from the southern edge of the summit. Small figures were moving slowly up the ridge—the Italians.

The seven men shouted, but their voices didn't carry. Then they threw rocks down, and finally the climbers looked up. They stood still for a few minutes, staring at the men on the summit. Then they slowly turned and began to go down.

Whymper's thoughts flew to Carrel down there with the Italians, and in his generous heart he forgave the guide. "He judged badly," the artist thought. "He

The Matterhorn appears impossible to climb.

should be standing here with us."

The successful mountaineers remained at the top for an hour. They were so happy that they danced around wildly. Croz set up a tent pole, which he had carried all the way from their camp, and tied his shirt to it. The day was fine. Down below, for miles around, people saw that flag. At Zermatt every man, woman, and child was out celebrating. Matterhorn the unconquerable had been conquered!

Hudson came up to Whymper, who was making a sketch of the summit and the great peaks around it.

"In what order shall we go down?" he asked.

Now, in descending a mountain, it is usual for the strongest guide to go last. In case of a slip, he can hold the rope fast. But young Hadow was so worn out that he needed both Croz and Hudson to help him. So it was decided that Croz, the best guide, should go first, Hadow second, Hudson third, then Douglas, with the elder Taugwalder last. Whymper and young Peter would go on another rope by themselves.

While the artist was finishing his sketch, Croz roped

On the summit.

up the five. Then someone remembered they had not left their names in the heap of stones they had piled up on the summit. Whymper hastily wrote them down, put the paper in a bottle, and ran to join the others, who had moved on. When he and young Peter caught up, they were already in the most difficult part of the descent.

Douglas said to Whymper, "Tie your line to old Taugwalder. I am afraid if there is a slip, he won't be able to hold without help."

Whymper did as he was asked, making a chain of the seven men. He failed to notice that Croz had made a terrible mistake. The rope which bound the first four men together was strong and sound, but the one that held Douglas, the fourth man, to Taugwalder was an old rope which had been taken along only for an emergency. For some reason Croz had used it instead of the second stout piece of rope carried by the party.

They were working down the rocky slope, one man moving at a time very carefully. In one spot, Croz found he had to lay down his ice ax while he placed each of Hadow's feet in the next step so that he should not slip. Suddenly, before Croz could pick up his ax and straighten up, Hadow's feet glided from under him. They struck Croz in the back and hurled him off into space. Hadow himself followed, and an instant later

Hudson was dragged after Hadow. Douglas, taken by surprise, failed to belay the rope around a rock. Next moment he too was snatched from the cliff.

The elder Taugwalder had heard Croz cry out when Hadow's feet struck him. He couldn't see what was happening below, but he reacted at once. He belayed the rope over a rock and braced himself for the jerk. Whymper and young Peter did the same. When the jerk came on them, they held. But the weak rope between Douglas and Taugwalder did not.

Taugwalder stared aghast at the torn end of rope in his hand. Then the three men crept forward a few steps and looked down. They saw Croz, Hadow, Hudson, and Douglas shooting down the steep slope on their backs, spreading out their hands to clutch at the rock. One by one they disappeared.

They were too stunned to move. For a whole hour they stood where they were. Young Peter seemed frozen to the rock he was gripping.

The rest of the descent was a nightmare. They spent the night on a bare slab and at daybreak continued on to Zermatt.

"What is the matter?" the hotelkeeper asked, frightened by Whymper's haggard face when he walked in.

"The Taugwalders and I have returned," Whymper replied in a dead voice.

The hotelkeeper burst into tears. He understood. A terrible price had been paid for the Matterhorn.

Rudi drives a piton (safety spike)
into a crack in the rock.
He will pass a rope through the
snap link.

Balancing themselves with great skill,
Rudi and his father climb
a steep "chimney" in the rocks.

If Rudi slips, the strain will come on the
link instead of on his father.

The training of a mountaineer

Emil Perren, famous Matterhorn guide, teaches his son Rudi the skills of mountaineering.

Rudi "ropes off" a steep cliff. Although this looks dangerous, it is the safest and fastest method of descending very steep rocks.

3 The Rockies

A hundred ranges in one

Turn the clock back sixty million years and watch the Rockies rise, jagged and new, all the way from the Arctic to our own Southwest!

It is a strange world into which the early mountains climb. Giant reptiles rule America. Dinosaurs walk the earth. Swimming reptiles sport in the seas. Flying reptiles sweep through the air.

Ages pass. Inch by inch the mountains shrink—four inches in a thousand years, perhaps. Sun and air, wind and rain and frost crack and chip and blast and wash the rock down. Finally thousands of millions of tons of

57

rock waste lie on the Great Plains and other neighboring lands. Streams, cutting deep valleys in the mountain-sides, carry other tons of rubbish to the seas. Then at last the rushing rivers rest. Lazily they wander over nearly level ground.

By now the world around the mountains has changed too. Gone are the giant reptiles. Mammals have taken their place. Horses and other hoofed animals graze on the prairies. Birds sing and flowers bloom. Elephants have wandered in from Asia.

Then again the earth labors. There where one day our West will be, the Rocky Mountain area is lifted up nearly a mile. And as it rises, the lazy streams awake. Once more they rush down a steep grade. Like so many giant buzz saws, they rip deep gaps through the uplifted mountains. All the big rivers and many of their tributaries saw gorges through the Rockies. They cut the steep, exciting canyons of today.

Now comes another change. The great Ice Age sets in. In the Rocky Mountains valley glaciers form. The glaciers give the mountains a final shaping, grinding and plowing and scraping them into pretty much the form they have today. Four times the glaciers advance and four times they retreat. When the ice goes for the last time, America is new again.

The animals are different now. Gone are the horse and the elephant. Vast herds of buffalo graze on the plains. Deer, elk, moose, and grizzly bear dwell in the thick forests with which the Rockies have clothed themselves. Clambering among the crags are bighorn sheep and ever-white mountain goats with a big hump on their shoulders. There are pronghorn antelope in the grassy valleys. The rivers of these mountains teem with

The towering Tetons of Wyoming are a challenge to mountaineers.

fish. Beaver build their dams in the streams. Blueberries spread high up on the slopes and raspberries, blackberries, and wild cranberries grow down below.

There are men here who hunt the beasts and gather in the fullness. When they have had good hunting, they bring offerings to the lords of the high places.

The Indians look at the Shining Mountains, as they call the ranges of our West. Half in wonder, half in fear, they watch the storm clouds cast their lightnings at the peaks. The Indians weave endless tales of how the mountains came to be.

The Rocky Mountains stretch all the way from

Winter in the Rockies starts early and ends late.

Range after range the Rockies rise—the roof of North America.

Alaska to New Mexico. In Canada the chain of peaks is unbroken, but farther south the Rockies are many chains with rolling tablelands between. It would be better to call our Rockies a hundred ranges in one—and, indeed, a hundred have been counted.

The line along the highest crests is called the Continental Divide. All the rivers on the western side of the Continental Divide empty into the Pacific Ocean. All the rivers on the eastern side empty into the Gulf of Mexico, Hudson Bay, or the Arctic Ocean.

In Canada the Rockies are very much like the Alps, and almost as high. Here are the same snowy peaks, the same quiet valleys, the same beautiful blue lakes.

Mountain climbers love the Canadian Rockies and some say they rival the Alps in beauty.

The United States Rockies, too, have variety and excitement. But one part of the region has more meaning for Americans than all the rest. For here are the mountains that stood directly in the westward path of American settlers, barring the way as if to say, "You shall not pass!"

Six great ranges make up this section of the Rockies —the Front or Rampart, the Park, Wasatch, Sangre de Cristo, San Juan, and Medicine Bow. Mainly they are in Colorado. But fingers jut north into Wyoming and south into New Mexico. This is a region bristling with giants. Here are some of the mightiest and most famous peaks in North America. Here stands Mount Elbert, 14,419 feet. Here are Pikes Peak and Longs Peak. More than fifty of the giants are at least 14,000 feet high. More than 1,500 get up to 10,000 feet and beyond.

It is a rugged region, but not all of it is so. Between the ranges lie wide, flat basins through which run the headwaters of four great rivers—the Colorado, the South Platte, the Arkansas, and the Rio Grande. The most exciting part of America's story of the West took place in and through and around these ranges and these basins.

Opening up the Rockies

See the Rockies in the 1830's! Indians are not the only men here now. In a hundred little mountain streams, white men are busy setting beaver traps. Beaver pelts are wanted for the big swaggering hats men wear.

They are hardy fellows, these mountain men, known for their skill with trap and rifle, famous for their know-how in the wilderness and the quick thinking that has often saved their lives. In the 1830's there are several hundred of them in the Rockies. Many have come in bands led by men like Jim Bridger, Tom Fitzpatrick, and Kit Carson.

Mountain men travel light. They don't take much with them, for they live mainly off their hunting. A rifle, a powder horn and lead for bullets. A knife for skinning. A hatchet and awl, a frypan and coffeepot. Blankets to sleep in. Traps. Pipe and tobacco.

It is a rough life, and those who have come alone will have only their pony and a mule or two for company. The Rockies are so vast that there isn't much chance of running into another trapper. A mountain man is much more apt to meet up with an Indian, and then the meeting is likely to be unpleasant. A mountain man has to be ever on his guard.

He has learned the Indian's woodcraft. He looks for signs of animals and signs of human beings. Is a blade of grass bent? Is there a hollow in the moss? He recognizes quickly what the signs mean. He thinks and acts fast. He has all the wild animal's wariness. And, like a wild animal, he is never lost. Put him down anywhere, and though he may be "confused" for a little while, he will soon find his way. He has the habit of remembering scenery. He writes the geography down in his mind.

For ten short years mountain men rule the Rockies, and then a change takes place. Beaver is no longer wanted, for tall silk hats have replaced the big swaggering ones. Most of the mountain men leave the Rockies.

The Rockies long were a barrier between east and west.

But they have shown the way, and now wagon trains roll over the great pass which mountain man Jim Bridger found. If Oregon Territory is to become part of the United States, settlers are needed there. In the 1840's there are plenty who want to go west. Mountain men act as guides on the Oregon Trail.

Clouds of dust from the turning wheels almost hide the travelers. Bull whips crack as the slow oxen plod up the valley of the North Platte, up the Sweetwater. The wagons cross the Rockies over South Pass, then press on. Every summer five to ten bands come through.

Suddenly in 1849 the traffic grows much heavier. Gold has been discovered in California and thousands dream of fortune. The gold-rushers are in a tearing hurry to get there. That first year some 12,000 wagons are strung out on the plains and in the High Rockies. Almost 30,000 people try to get through the mountains to California. Eight thousand wagons go over South Pass before the year is out.

A few more years and gold is discovered in the Rockies themselves. From 1859 to 1861 there is plenty

Roads in the Rockies follow trails of the mountain men.

of gold in Colorado for anyone willing to dig for it. The rush to the Rockies is a stampede. Then in 1876 silver is found in Colorado too, and even more prospectors pour into the mountains.

California all this time has been cut off from the East. It is way over at the other end of nowhere, and wagons take forever to reach it. "How about a railroad?" people ask.

But can railroads cross the great Rockies? Is it possible for trains to operate the year around when mountain winters are so cruel and snows so heavy?

Men like John C. Frémont go to the Rockies in dead of winter to search out routes for the railroads. The explorers pay a terrible price for their boldness. But in time the rails are laid. In 1869 the first transcontinental railroad is finished.

It is startling to look back, startling to realize that it took less then a century to tame the wild Rockies. Today highways span them, railways cross and recross them. Towns dot the ranges. The basins are fruitful farms. It is hard to believe that just a little while ago the mountain men were trapping here.

Climbers and mountaineers

For a long time, the Rockies were just mountains to plunder, to get around, or to get through. For most of those who went West in the early years were trappers, traders, pioneers, homesteaders, fortune seekers. They had neither time nor thought for mountaineering.

Today the Rockies are forever being climbed and explored, and often by people who are not expert mountaineers—campers, hikers, and tourists. Though the peaks are high, many of them are not difficult to climb. Nearly all have one or more easy ways to reach the summit, and only a few call for great mountaineering

A mountaineer "ropes off" down a steep cliff in the Canadian Rockies. He must lean back with his feet braced against the rock wall.

skill. Everywhere the trails are blazed. So almost anyone who wants to make the effort can get to the top. Experienced mountaineers can go to the difficult mountains, or they may tackle an easy mountain by some hard route.

Glacier National Park in northern Montana is one of the regions that draw mountain climbers. Here in the Lewis Range there are heights that present a challenge worthy of skilled climbers. And this is even more true of the wild Beartooth Mountains in southern Montana. Granite Peak is the highest in the range and a very difficult peak to climb. But it has been conquered.

South of the Yellowstone is the Teton Range. Every summer hordes of climbers, including many boys and girls, come to test their courage and endurance in the Tetons. There is even a mountaineering school on the spot, where two of America's best climbers teach. The Tetons deserve their fine reputation as a learning ground, for they vary in difficulty—and none is child's play. Grand Teton, the highest peak in the range, can be climbed by a number of different routes. The route up the north face is one of the hardest climbs in the

Climbers attempt one of Alaska's unmapped mountain peaks.

United States. It has been done only a few times.

For those who want out-of-the-way mountains, as fresh as when they were first discovered, the Wind River Range in Wyoming is tempting. The Wind Rivers with their glaciers make you think of the Alps. These mountains are so secluded that few people go there, and some of the peaks have never been climbed. In the Sangre de Cristo Range there are peaks that call for great mountaineering skill. Farther south still, the San Juans are even wilder and more exciting.

Americans are enthusiastic about mountain climbing— and not only in the Rockies. They climb wherever there are mountains to climb. The White Mountains in New England are very popular. The Sierra Nevada and the Cascades attract thousands. Even in far-off Alaska, where the conditions are arctic, mountaineering goes on. There seems to be no mountain challenge so great that men will turn aside from it.

It is in Alaska that Mount McKinley, the top of our continent, stands. This peak, too, has been conquered. And the story of meeting that challenge is one of the strangest in the whole story of mountaineering.

The strange conquest of Mount McKinley

Mount McKinley is a very great single mountain—one of the greatest. Starting up from low country, it rises three and a half miles to become the tipmost top of North America.

In the year 1903, Dr. Frederick A. Cook came to explore around Mount McKinley. Dr. Cook had done a lot of traveling on ice and snow. In 1891–1892 he had been surgeon for the Peary Arctic Expedition. Later he had gone to the Antarctic with a Belgian expedition. Now he wanted very much to have the fame of standing on the summit of the highest peak in

Mount McKinley—fifteen miles away—soars
three miles above the mountaineers in the foreground.

North America.

In 1906 he made the attempt. He couldn't get anywhere near the top. His party floundered in the trackless wilderness and could find no approach to the higher levels.

In September, after the party broke up, Dr. Cook came back to the base bringing with him just one man. The man was Edward Barrille, who had been a packer for him. The two disappeared into the wilderness. A few weeks later they came out again. Now the doctor had a thrilling story to tell and photographs to back it up.

Headlines told the exciting news. MOUNT MCKINLEY CLIMBED. BROOKLYN DOCTOR STANDS ON HIGHEST PEAK OF CONTINENT. Long columns of print were broken with pictures of the famous explorer—and with photographs he had taken on the summit.

It was a glorious time for Dr. Cook (though not nearly so grand as a few years later when he claimed to have discovered the North Pole). Article after article about his climbing feat appeared in magazines. The famous man lectured here and lectured there. Then he wrote a book, *To the Top of the Continent*. In it he told the story of the ascent and described the view from the top. Cook dwelt on the "dazzling whiteness of the frosted granite blocks" of the summit. And he printed a picture of the rocks.

But the Alaskan prospectors—known as "sourdoughs"
—were not taken in. They knew you couldn't climb the
peak from the south side as Cook claimed he had. On
the south the mountain was mostly rock cliffs. And you
couldn't climb it in the month of September from any
side at all. Every condition of weather and mountain
was wrong in September. It was their united opinion
that Cook had invented his tale.

In the fall of 1909, in a saloon in Fairbanks, a group
of sourdoughs were discussing the doctor's story of his
climb.

"He sure took pains to fake it," said gold miner
Tom Lloyd. "It would be easier to *climb* McKinley than
do all that faking."

"I don't believe it," Bill McPhee observed. "I don't
believe any living man could climb it."

"For two cents I'd climb it myself," Lloyd boasted.

McPhee gave a laugh. "You're too old to climb it,
Tom, and too fat."

"Well," Lloyd replied good-naturedly, "anyway I
could *find* men who will do it."

McPhee set down his glass and drew the back of
his hand across his handlebar moustache. "I'd willingly
give $500 to have McKinley climbed," he said, "and
prove Cook never did it."

Lloyd set his glass down too. "I don't mind going in on it myself," he said. "I have dogs and horses coming out from my mines in the McKinley district after supplies. When they arrive with some of my men, we'll see about this climbing-party business."

Gust Peterson, the saloon keeper, chipped in with another $500. E. W. Griffin, a wholesale liquor dealer of Chena, contributed $500 more.

Excitement grew. All sorts of professional men wanted to go along. "This isn't a scientific expedition," Lloyd told them all. "We don't want any publicity. We don't care if nobody ever hears about this climb. All we want to do is show up that fellow Cook for our own satisfaction. Yes—and prove to ourselves we're just as husky as we ever were."

The party that set out in February consisted of four men who knew nothing at all about mountaineering. They included Tom Lloyd and his mining partner, Big Bill Taylor. The third man was Charlie McGonagall, who had been a mail driver for years. The fourth was Pete Andersen—big Swede Andersen, who worked for Lloyd and Taylor and was probably the strongest man in the North.

Never was an expedition outfitted like this one. As a reporter wrote later in the *New York Times*, the party "took less junk with them than people in the East

would take along for a one-day outing in the hills."
They carried no scientific equipment. Their most com-
plicated instrument was a $5 camera. They didn't even
take an ice ax. Each man carried a pike—a long pole
with metal on the end. As for food, they had just
what any miner would take along—bacon and beans
and flour. They would make their own sourdough
bread.

Lloyd led the party straight to the Muldrow Glacier.
Now, all who had ever tried to climb Mount McKinley
had passed around the snout of the Muldrow, for they
had no idea that the glacier was the one possible approach. They didn't realize that it turned and twisted

The Muldrow Glacier (at right) was a key to Mount McKinley.

Mountaineers probe a snow bridge over a tremendous crevasse in the Muldrow Glacier.

and led up until it came to the only ridge by which the upper glacier, or Grand Basin, could be reached and the summits gained. Lloyd had long ago discovered this when he hunted wild sheep in the foothills.

The party put on their snowshoes. With dogs and sleds they hauled their few supplies to the head of the Muldrow. On the ridge above the glacier they made camp. It was Lloyd who got the meal. "Boys," he said, "McPhee was right. I'm too fat for climbing. You do the prospecting up the mountain and I'll keep camp."

Day after day Taylor, McGonagall, and Andersen toiled up the gigantic, steep, knife-edge Karsten Ridge. They never once thought they were doing anything out of the ordinary.

When the tea and coffee ran out, they just kept boiling the same grounds over and over. When Bill Taylor fell in a crevasse, his pike caught across the top and he swung himself out. Pete Andersen froze a toe, but it didn't slow him down. "That Swede is a tower of strength," Lloyd confided to his partner. "Mount McKinley must be 21,000 feet. But if it was twice as high, I believe the Swede would go to the top of it."

For a whole month they worked getting ready for the last attack. Then at two in the morning on April 3, they strapped great climbing irons on their moccasins and started up. Besides their pikes, they carried an unusual burden—a 14-foot flagstaff. At 18,500 feet, McGonagall turned back. But Pete Andersen and Bill Taylor, in one superhuman push—which climbers have never stopped wondering at—climbed to the top of the North Peak. There, at 19,470 feet, they planted their flagstaff.

The South Peak was 850 feet higher. It was also two miles away, with a 1500-foot-deep pass between. But anyway the climbers thought the North Peak was the best place for their flagpole. It could be seen, they fondly supposed, through a telescope from Fairbanks, 150 miles away. Taylor and Andersen nailed a board to the pole with the four names on it and the date— April 3, 1910.

Then they started down. In just a day and a half the party covered the distance it had taken them a month to do going up—another astonishing feat that still impresses mountaineers.

And Cook?

There was no question in the minds of the sourdoughs that he had never climbed the mountain. For there was only one logical approach, the one they had taken. That approach called for snowshoes. You couldn't move on the Muldrow without them. And Cook had never once mentioned snowshoes in his book.

The party of sourdoughs had shown the way up the mountain. Now it wasn't long before the true summit was won. In 1913 Archdeacon Stuck of the Yukon led a party of mountaineers to the top of the South Peak. He proved beyond doubt that Cook had never been to the top.

There were no "frosted granite blocks of dazzling whiteness" there. Above 19,000 feet Mount McKinley was all permanent snow and ice. The shape of the South Peak was nothing like the photograph Cook had printed as "The Top of Our Continent." Nor was the view from the summit such as he had described. As the sourdoughs had suspected, and as Barrille confessed, the famous photograph had been taken on a little peak in the foothills.

A hundred yards from the true top (South Peak) of Mount McKinley.

4 The Andes

Backbone of South America

High above white peaks, the condor wheels in circles on his mighty wings. He is the only living creature in those skies. Far below him on the high plateau the llama grazes. Those two—the condor and the llama—tell you where you are. The snowy mountains stretching for five thousand miles, from the Caribbean to Cape Horn, are the Andes.

Outside of Asia, no mountains are higher than these. There are fifty peaks in the Andes over 20,000 feet high. Forty-six of them are higher than our great Mount McKinley. Chimborazo, which Edward Whymper

A sea of peaks in the Andes.

climbed in 1880, was long thought to be the highest mountain in the world. That dead—or maybe sleeping—volcano was the highest mountain that had yet been climbed. But Chimborazo is not even the loftiest peak in the Andes. Aconcagua is higher still.

Studded with smoking volcanoes, the snowy backbone of South America hugs the Pacific. The Andes run so close to the ocean that most of the way there is just the narrowest of narrow strips between the mountains and the sea. The big belly of the continent lies on the other side, with the Amazon streaming through it. Scientists tell us the mountains made that mighty river. They say the Amazon basin was once a salt-water gulf. Then the Andes rose. They shut off the gulf at its western end, tipped the salt water out into the Atlantic, and fed fresh water in. They turned the gulf into earth's grandest river.

Beautiful Chimborazo, long considered the world's highest mountain.

The Andes made the Amazon and they keep it full. The moisture-laden winds that sweep from the Atlantic can't get over the heights. They crown the peaks with snow. Melting, the snow joins the streaming rain water on the east side of the range and goes into the thousand rivers that carry tribute to the Amazon. Much of the Pacific coast, meantime, is left dry, with hardly a drop of rain.

Because the Andes run north and south through the whole length of South America, there are great contrasts in climate. In Ecuador, which is at the equator and has a high altitude, it is forever spring. Here the sun shines without ever scorching. Nearly everything grows. On the lower slopes it is palms and bananas, oranges and cocoa. A little higher up it is coffee, quinine, rubber, tobacco, pineapples, and citrus fruits. In the mountain valleys grains and vegetables of all kinds flourish. Pastures climb right up to the snow line.

Ecuador is so rich and bracing that the Indians say they are never sick until they die. Lucky Ecuador! It is the only part of the Andes where one can say that. It is the only part that is joyous. The farther south you go from here, the gloomier the mountain region gets. In Peru it is bitter cold even on the lower slopes. In northern Chile, on the other hand, in the region of the Atacama Desert, it is hot and dry. Pata-

*At a height of 18,800 feet in the Andes, a climber
blows up his air mattress.*

gonia, farther south, is the gloomiest part of all. There
are places in Patagonia where it storms 300 days in
the year. From Patagonia the picture you carry away
is of snow swirling around mighty peaks.

You could look the world over without finding richer
mountains than the Andes. They are a vast treasure
house of gold, silver, copper, tin, iron, lead, quicksilver,
coal. The largest emeralds in the world are mined
here. But it is not for their mineral wealth the Andes
are most famous. Not for the "Irish" potato or for the
tomato developed here. Not for the lima bean, the
peanut, and quinine which surely were born here.

Most of all the Andes are renowned for the Incas
of Peru.

Empire in the mountains

The Spaniards who conquered Peru came there in
1532 to get gold. It was gold and more gold that they
sent back to their ruler in Spain. But they saw also the
Kingdom of the Sun, the vast, organized empire which
the Indians had built in the Andes. The Spaniards could
hardly believe what their eyes showed them.

They saw great cities built of stone, temples, palaces,
forts, and aqueducts. Terraced farms climbed high up
steep slopes, and irrigation kept them green. The Spaniards saw weavers working rich patterns into cloth of
llama, alpaca, and vicuña wool. They saw potters

Ruins of Machu Picchu, an Inca city
in the clouds, discovered by Hiram Bingham in 1911.

shaping dishes that were works of art. The Spaniards saw an empire running so smoothly that every man, woman, and child—25,000,000 in all—had enough to eat, enough to wear, and a house to live in. They saw what we, in the modern world, still only dream about.

Why did this happen in the mountains of Peru?

Nobody is sure of the answer. If you were to see the part of the Andes which was the Inca world, you would not believe that such a land could produce such a wonder-working people.

Start from the Pacific. The narrow coast before you is a desert where it never rains. Hundreds of little waterways drop down from the mountains, but in most of them there is no glint of water. Only in flood season will all the streams run full.

The mountains are brown and barren. And because there is no rain to wear them down, the foothills are just as steep as the peaks. The peaks themselves are terrifying. Till you get up to 5,000 feet, there isn't a bit of green on the mountains. It is cold and windy here much of the time. Storms are frequent. Above the band of green lies everlasting snow.

Climb the ridge to the top. Now you will see that in Peru the Andes consist principally of two chains of mountains with a great plateau between. The plateau lies from one and a half to two miles above sea level.

Here and there it is broken by ridges. Bowls and valleys are closed in by barren heights. To the south the plateau gets higher, bleaker, very windy, very cold. Here lies Lake Titicaca, the highest big lake in the world, half as big as Lake Ontario.

Cross now to the other side of the farther chain. This side of the Andes that faces the Atlantic is very different from the side that faces the Pacific. Instead of drought, there is endless rain. Instead of too little, there is too much water. Below the snow line, down at about 6,000 feet, lies the humid, hot montaña, matted

The terraced farms of the Incas are one of the world's wonders. They rise like giant steps almost to the mountaintops.

and choked with growing things. This is where the great rivers start down with a wild plunge to join the Amazon. This is the beginning of the steaming jungle.

Such was the world of the Incas. Their empire covered one quarter of South America—and much of it was as high as Mont Blanc.

Though it seems unbelievable to us, the Incas met the challenge of the Andes. They farmed the mountainsides, the deserts and plateaus. They fed 25,000,000 people. They developed a system that worked perfectly.

There was, of course, no contact between the ruler and the ruled. The workers tilled the land, herded the llamas, mined the metals, worked at the crafts, and performed a hundred services. Two-thirds of all they created went to the king and the "church," of which he was head. He had two hundred palaces filled with riches which their hands had made. The walls of those palaces were covered with gold and silver, studded with jewels. Yet in his journeys he never heard complaints that someone was hungry, cold, or shelterless. The people produced enough for all.

Color, glitter, glamor, pomp—they dazzled everyone. The Inca people were awed by them. The Spaniards were awed too. But something else impressed them more. Of all the marvels in this marvelous empire of the Andes, nothing amazed them more than the royal mountain road.

The Incas had other roads. One ran for 2,520 miles along the coast. There were special military roads, as well as roads on which troops of llamas carried gold. But the royal road, which ran for 3,250 miles along the grand plateau, was the most wonderful of all. The boldest of our engineers today marvel at the daring way in which the Inca builders met the problems of that road.

It passed over mountains buried in snow. It climbed precipices by stairways hewn in sheer cliffs. Galleries were cut for miles through rock. Ravines were filled up with stone. Rivers were crossed by bridges that hung from aloe cables thick as a man's body. One of these bridges spanned the frightful gorge of the Apurimac River. The walls of that gorge are 150 feet apart. The winds there are so strong that the bridge swayed like a hammock at times. But it held. It was built so well that it lasted 500 years before it plunged into the gorge.

The great Inca roads held the empire together. Speeding along them, the king's swift relay-runners brought him word of happenings near and far. In a week's time he had the news from a thousand miles away. Was there rebellion anywhere? Did some chieftain withhold tribute? He gave the word, and in a matter of hours the Inca armies were on the march.

Mountain dwellers of today

In the little shut-in valleys of the Andes, you can
see today the descendants of the ancient Indian people
who won and lost so much. They speak the same
Quechua tongue their ancestors spoke. There are not
so many of these pure-blooded Indians as there were
in the olden days. Instead of the 25,000,000 who lived
here under the Inca rule, there are perhaps 5,000,000.

The Andes Mountains are hard to live in. But the
Indians belong to these walled-in valleys where the
grim mountains look down. They want no other world
than the simple one they know. There is the shady

slope—that's for one crop. There is the sunny side—that's for another. There is the torrent, or the lake, and high above all is the peak. On the summit dwells *Inti*, the all-powerful creator. In the depths live the demons. Though the Indians have been baptized and go to church, each valley has as many gods as there are mountains shutting it in.

Just as in the old days, the people are farmers. But now they are desperately poor. Most of them don't own their land, and they have to give their landlord two-thirds of what they produce. They live in houses of unbaked brick, with a roof of thatch or tile. Gloomy and cold inside, their hut barely protects them from the fierce mountain winds. There is no window, no chimney—just a rude hearth made of stones. There is scarcely any furniture—just a few mats, a few dishes. From the ceiling, bean sticks and ears of maize hang down. The food is mainly frozen potatoes, quinoa (a grain something like rice), and corn.

The Indians have donkeys now. But the llama which their ancestors bred from the wild guanaco is closer to them. The creature asks for so little! It will live on clumps of ichu grass, which grows everywhere on the Andean plateau. And the llama does so much for the Indians! It gives them wool for clothing and ropes and cords. Its hide makes leather, its flesh is food, and its

Although the Indians have the donkey now, the llama is nearer to their hearts.

bones have many uses. For in the high mountains there are no trees. Here all sorts of household objects are made of llama bone. Even native flutes are made of it. Llama dung is fuel. A big pile of it lies near every hut in the high mountains.

The Indians are desperately poor, but the spirit of the Incas is in them still. They show it in the color of their festivals and dances. They show it in the skilled work of their hands. When they make music, they play on the same instruments their ancestors used—flutes, pipes, clay trumpets, drums, rattles.

In the market places you see the Indians wearing the tall hats which the Spaniards taught them to wear. If you look close, under the tall hat you will often see an Inca cap. It shows you the old is not forgotten. It is there, just under the new.

Whymper climbs the highest active volcano

The peaks of the Andes are magnificent, and the volcanoes of Ecuador are perhaps the most impressive of all. Ecuador has some forty of them. Though most are dead and four or five appear to be sleeping, three are very much alive. Cotopaxi and its two neighbors come pretty near holding the world's record for fireworks. In all South America there is nothing more exciting to see than these peaks with smoke pouring from their craters.

Cotopaxi—19,498 feet—stands only 43 miles south of the equator. Yet it is so high that it is crowned

Ecuador's Sangay—perhaps the most active of all volcanoes—sometimes shoots great rocks eight miles into the air.

with snow and ice and even has a glacier 500 feet from the top. It is the world's highest active volcano. When Edward Whymper saw it, he wanted to climb it immediately.

After the tragedy on the Matterhorn, Whymper had gone through a terrible time. He couldn't get out of his mind the image of his four companions shooting down the mountainside. People thought he would never climb again. But he kept on.

In 1879 and 1880 Whymper was in the Andes. He had no English companion, nor did he want any. But he did have two Swiss guides with him. One was Jean-Antoine Carrel—the same Carrel who had left Whymper fifteen years before to join the Italians climbing the Matterhorn. The other man was Carrel's cousin Louis.

The two guides didn't want to climb Cotopaxi. They weren't used to smoking volcanoes. Weren't there plenty of other peaks to climb?

Whymper tried to rouse their interest. He began to tell them what he knew about the volcano. Cotopaxi was always causing trouble. Just two years earlier, he said, there had been a big eruption. Lava had poured over the lip of the crater. It had sent a flood of water, ice, rock, and mud down the mountainside, laying waste everything in its path. It had swept away factories, houses, and farms. It had destroyed roads and bridges.

Months before the disaster, Cotopaxi had started to act up. Columns of smoke sometimes rose 1,000 feet above the cone, and winds carried the black dust wherever they blew. At night the vapor was lit up by the glowing lava inside the crater. Late in June an immense black column rose about twice as high as the cone. Everything was normal again early next morning. But at 6:30 another enormous column rose from the crater. The dust drifted as far as Quito, thirty miles to the north. At noontime it was as dark as night in the city.

"Meantime at ten that morning," Whymper said,

"people in the town of Mulalo looked up at the summit and saw lava pouring through gaps in the lip of
the crater. The lava was bubbling and steaming like
the froth of a pot that suddenly boils over. A few minutes later the whole volcano was swallowed up in smoke
and steam. Out of the darkness there rose a moaning
noise that grew into a roar. And then down the mountain came the flood of water, ice, mud and rock.

"The scene on that cone," Whymper went on, "must
have surpassed anything that has been seen by man.
When that bubbling lava poured out on the slopes, the
snow and ice must instantly have turned to steam, and
the lava was exploded sky high. Then it fell down
again on the cone, bounded in great leaps, and plowed
up the mountain like a cannonball. What wonder,"
he ended, "that huge chunks of glacier were carried
five miles from the mountain?"

The Carrels thought about it. Then Jean-Antoine
spoke up. "You have raised within me a great desire
to look into this animal," he said.

So they went up. It was an easy climb, for the slope
wasn't steep. The snow began only above 15,400 feet.
Before long the three men were pitching their tent on
the ash of the volcano. For the first time in their lives,
they found themselves pleasantly warm on a high
mountainside.

The final ascent from their camp next day was easy. By noon they were at the crater. Whymper hurried to the edge and looked eagerly in. To his disappointment, he could see nothing. The crater was nearly filled with smoke and steam. It drifted here and there and hid everything from sight. He could barely get a glimpse of the opposite side, and the bottom was a total mystery.

Suddenly a roar from the depths told them the volcano was very much alive. Before anyone could say a word, steam was billowing all around them. They had agreed beforehand what they should do if there was an eruption. They were to drop everything and run. But when the roar and the steam came, curiosity held them rooted to the spot.

After a while Whymper said, "Probably nothing more is going to happen. It is no use to stay here now. We must come back when it is dark."

They waited till night had fairly set in before they went up again. The cold air was very still, but from time to time the stillness was broken by the deadened roar of steam blasts as they escaped. Vapor still filled the crater. Now there was a strong glow, however, on the under side of the steam clouds. Whymper crawled to the lip and lay down. While Jean-Antoine held his legs, he peered into the unknown.

A volcano that blew its top. This is the crater of Volcano de Fuego in Guatemala.

Everything was visible. Vapor no longer hid any part of the crater.

What Whymper saw was an oval measuring about half a mile one way and a quarter of a mile the other. The rim was rugged, uneven, notched, and cracked. The sides of the crater were made of cliffs, some of them steep, others sloping. Some had snow on them, and some looked as if they might be crusted over with sulphur. Here and there smoke belched from deep caverns. Halfway down, the cracks and chasms in the walls shone with a ruddy light.

And this is how it was all the way down. Precipice and slope, precipice and slope continued right down to the bottom, with more and more fiery cracks the lower he looked. The bottom, Whymper judged, must be

1,200 feet below where he lay leaning over the rim. And there at the bottom was the cause of all the light and glow—a bright circle about one-tenth the width of the crater. This was the pipe of the volcano, its tie with the lower regions. The pipe was filled with molten, glowing lava.

Now a great noise sounded, and vapor came billowing up from below. But Whymper didn't move. He couldn't tear his eyes from that bright, roughly circular spot that went down—who knew how far?—into the earth.

He pictured to himself that time when the crater had overflowed. He was trying to imagine the power that could raise millions of tons of boiling rock from the bowels of the earth, overflowing that vast crater almost four miles above the sea. How puny man seemed here on the edge of this fiery wonder! How little he knew about the gigantic forces that had first lifted the high Andes and then set volcanoes on their shoulders! How little man knew of this strange earth he trod so confidently and called his own!

A voice behind him recalled Whymper to himself. He had forgotten he was not alone.

"You said something, Jean-Antoine?"

"I did. Let me look inside the animal now."

Reluctantly Whymper backed down and they changed places on the rim.

5 The Himalayas

Greatest mountains of all

"He who has once looked on these incomparable mountains must dream of them to the end of his days."

A great mountaineer said that about the Himalayas, and nobody will dispute it. The Himalayas dwarf all other ranges. In these great wrinkles on the face of Asia are hundreds of peaks higher than the highest peak on any other continent. Three are higher by a mile.

Like a great bow with the ends pointing upward, the Himalayas curve above India, shutting it off on the north. The arc is 100 to 150 miles wide. From end to end it measures 1,500 miles. It would take all the

mountains of Europe together to equal this mass of rock
and ice.

You must look at the Himalayas from the plains of
India to see their full height. For on the north the
mountains back up against the plateau of Tibet; and
that plateau is itself some 16,000 feet high.

Along the border between Tibet and Nepal stand the

Giants of the Himalayas.

loftiest peaks of all. Here is Everest, earth's highest peak, 29,028 feet. Close by are the third, fourth, and fifth highest mountains—Kangchenjunga, Lhotse, and Makalu. But K2, second highest mountain in the world, is not here. K2 belongs to a subrange of the Himalayas, the Karakoram, at the west end of the bow.

These are giants that strike awe into all who look upon them. For not only are the peaks high. The whole range is still so young that the peaks are terribly steep and sharp. Time has barely started to plane them down. It will take many thousands of years to blunt those pointed tops, to smooth those steep sides, to widen those ice-choked valleys.

Of course, the mountains are covered with eternal snow. And that is what the name means—Himalaya, "Abode of Snow." Great rivers drain the slopes of the Himalayas. The Ganges, India's sacred river, starts in a waterfall that pours directly from a glacier.

There are high passes in the mountains. Right near Everest is one of the most famous—the pass of Nangpa La. It is between Tibet and Nepal. The pass crosses the Himalayas at 19,000 feet. High though it is, it has been used from ancient times right down to the present. Caravans wind through the jungle valleys of the south. They go up, up, up to the pass, carrying into Tibet cloth and spices and small manufactured goods from

K2, also known as Mount Godwin-Austen, is the second highest mountain in the world.

India and Nepal. Back the other way they come with salt and wool, the great products of the plateau.

Sometimes herds of yaks come over the pass from Tibet. This is the important animal for all the peoples of the high Himalayas. Ages ago the Tibetans tamed it along with the two-humped camel, and it has become the great staple of life. The yak is as important to the Tibetans as the llama is to the Indians who live in the mountains of Peru. The yak gives almost everything the Tibetans need to feed them and keep them warm. It gives them wool for clothing, leather for shoes. It gives them milk, from which butter and cheese are made. Yak dung is used for fuel. But only rarely is a yak killed for meat. This is Buddhist country where the killing of animals is frowned on. Even the shoes are made from hides of yaks that have died a natural death.

In these high regions, life is hard. The land is harsh and stony. The weather is bitter most of the year, and the wind blows nearly all the time. Wheat grows up to 8,000 or 10,000 feet, barley and potatoes up to 14,000. Grass climbs up to 18,000, so that yaks graze close beside the glaciers and under the walls of the great mountains. In Nepal, in the district of Solo Khumbu near the pass of Nangpa La, there are no towns, no stores. The ordinary village house is made of rough mountain stone with a shingle roof and windows without glass. The house clings to the mountainside like another rock. Most have two floors. The yaks, goats, and sheep live on the ground floor.

In such a house as this the world-famous Sherpa, Tenzing Norgay, lived as a boy. He remembers how crowded the family was, all packed together in a small space, with the noise and the smell and the smoke from cooking. "But we were happy and contented," he tells us in his wonderful book, "because we did not know there was any other way to live."

They didn't know because for centuries the mountain wilderness between India and Tibet was shut away from the Western world. The Mongolian Sherpas, who long before Tenzing's day had come to Nepal from Tibet, had never seen Westerners. They had never heard of men who wanted to climb mountains. And nobody in Europe had heard of such a people as the Sherpas.

In the early nineteenth century, very few Europeans knew anything about Tibet. And the Himalayan peaks were not shown on maps. Nobody visited them. Geographers didn't know which peak was which or how high any of them were.

Help from the Sherpas

It was the British who finally measured the height of the Himalayan peaks and put them on the map. That's why the world's highest mountain bears an Englishman's name. The British didn't know what the local name was and named it Everest after the head of the Indian Measurement Service. By the time they found out that Chomolungma was the right name, it was too late to change.

Chomolungma, "Goddess-Mother-of-the-World"—that's what the scholars said it meant. But Tenzing Norgay, who tended his father's yaks in the mountain's shadow, says that to him as a boy it meant Mountain-So-High-No-Bird-Can-Fly-Over-It.

In 1933 a man-made bird flew over Everest.

In 1953 two human beings stood on its top. It had taken eleven expeditions and hundreds of men to conquer the highest peak on earth.

But why expeditions? And why so many?

One of the first things Himalayan climbers learned is that you cannot tackle the high peaks alone, or with just a guide, or with a friend or two. In the first place, the giants hide themselves in such remote wilderness that you can't even get to them alone. It takes careful planning and many porters to reach the mountains with everything you will need—tents and sleeping bags and food and mattresses and clothing and stoves and fuel and cameras and oxygen tanks.

When you do get there, you find that every problem of mountaineering is many times more difficult in the Himalayas. Just because the mountains are so huge. There is more rock, more ice, the avalanches are bigger, the ridges are longer. And the weather is just about the worst there is. India is so hot and Tibet so cool that the peaks are battered by fierce storms. When blizzards and gales suddenly arise, it is a major problem just to keep from freezing.

Only a few weeks in late spring and a few weeks in

early fall are suitable for climbing. But the Himalayan peaks are so high that they cannot be climbed quickly. Man was not made to live on the heights where there is so little oxygen to breathe. He can exist and function above a certain height only if he gets used to it gradually. And even then he can't stay on the heights for long. He begins to see double. He doesn't react quickly. At times it seems easier to die than to take another step. Oxygen is a help, but it can't be used constantly. Besides, an oxygen tank is so heavy that it may become a burden instead of a help.

So a high peak in the Himalayas has to be tackled by a team. Only two or three or four of the strongest climbers make the last spurt to the top. They have to be spared and saved for that last great effort. The rest of the team set up a whole series of camps, each one higher than the one before. And the last camp must be close enough to the top for the final spurt.

In the Himalayas the grand moments are few. Most of the time it is grinding work. It is carrying endless loads up and down. So the question of porters is of first importance.

"If we had not found the Sherpas, we never could have won the summits," Himalayan climbers say.

For none of the other local people would go up the

Winding up and down the mountainside for days, men and mules carry supplies for the assault on a Himalayan peak.

Four Sherpa porters take a "standing rest."

mountains. They were afraid of the demons who guarded
the heights. Only the Sherpas were not afraid. Proudly
they took up the profession of porters. They carried
bigger loads and took them farther and higher than any
other men in the world. They carried their packs on
glaciers and icefalls, up ridges and precipices, through
blizzards and avalanches. On most big climbs of this
century, Sherpas set up the highest camps.

Nor did they feel that their duty ended there. They

took good care of their "sahibs," as they called the climbers. The Sherpas cooked for them, brought them their tea, looked after their equipment, saw to it that they were comfortable in their tents. They did this not only because they were paid for it but because they were part of a team.

Many of them gave their lives. More Sherpas died on the Himalayas than mountaineers from all other nations put together. Seven Sherpas were killed on Everest. Fifteen died on Nanga Parbat. On dozens of other mountains, Sherpas were lost in storms and avalanches, fell to their death, or died of cold or exhaustion.

A Sherpa beside an expedition tent high in the Himalayas.

Sometimes Sherpas died trying to save the life of a "sahib." Occasionally a Sherpa chose to die rather than leave his "sahib" to die alone.

Over the years the Sherpas learned the skills of mountaineering. They helped to find ·routes, cut steps, handle ropes, choose camp sites. In 1952 a Sherpa stepped out from the ranks of porters and became a climber second to none. It happened on the first Swiss expedition to Mount Everest. In each of three major Everest expeditions he was a key figure. Many believe Everest would not yet have been won had it not been for him. Everest is Tenzing Norgay's mountain more than any other man's.

Attempts on Mount Everest

In May 1922, sixty Sherpas, a hundred Tibetans, and more than three hundred pack animals took part in an unsuccessful British attempt on Everest. It was the second Mount Everest expedition. More were to follow.

The first had come the year before just to explore a way to the summit. The mountain had seemed almost too big a challenge for man. George Mallory, the leading spirit of the party, had climbed to a higher point on Everest than the highest peak in the Rockies. And still Everest soared up two miles more.

Its shape was clear. Everest was a pyramid with three great faces and three main ridges. To climb the faces was out of the question. But the northeast ridge seemed possible, and for nearly thirty years every expedition to Everest followed this route laid out by Mallory. In 1924 Mallory himself made a fatal attempt to reach the top. He was last seen at 28,000 feet—and never again.

Tenzing got his first chance at the mountain in 1935, on the fifth expedition, when he was twenty-one years old. He was miserable that the British could make no

Sherpa porters at the start of an ascent.

try for the top. For Sherpas have their dreams too, and Tenzing's yearning to stand on top of great Chomolungma was as strong as Mallory's.

Twice more in the 1930's Tenzing went to Everest. He became a Tiger. That was what the British called the Sherpas who climbed highest. In 1938 he came near losing his life in an avalanche, but he climbed up to 27,200 feet. With snow almost to their armpits, the party had to give up. Tenzing didn't know that the Second World War was coming and that fourteen years would pass before he got his next real chance at Chomolungma.

In 1950 the Chinese moved into Tibet and closed the doors to Westerners. At the same time Nepal opened her doors. What this meant was that any expedition to Everest must now come from the other side—the south side. It meant starting all over again to find a new route.

That year and the next the British tried. They saw a possible way. It lay through a deep, snowy valley that led right up to Mount Lhotse, Everest's neighbor. They would go part way up Lhotse, veer off to the left, get on Everest, and follow the east ridge to the top. But the first step was to get into the valley, and that wasn't easy.

To do it, you had to go along the Khumbu Glacier

and up a very steep, high icefall. This was a tumbled mass of ice that plunged down to the glacier through a narrow passage between Everest and another neighbor —Nuptse.

In 1951 the British managed to get up the terrible icefall, but almost at the top they were stopped by a great crevasse. It was much too wide to jump. It was so deep you couldn't see the bottom. And it stretched from one side of the icefall to the other. They couldn't get across.

The Nepalese had said they would allow only one Western nation in at a time, and the following year the Swiss had been promised a turn. They got in touch with Tenzing, who had climbed lesser mountains with them in 1947. Would he come along as sirdar, leader of the Sherpas?

Tenzing was overjoyed. He was going back to Chomolungma. He was going back with the Swiss, the people he liked climbing with most of all. And as sirdar —the highest honor a Sherpa could look to.

He chose his porters with great care and marched them off to join the Swiss. And now for the first time he met the man who would be his companion on the heights and his best friend for all time. It was Raymond Lambert, a famous Swiss guide. Tenzing noticed at once that Lambert's boots looked strangely short. Later he

Nuptse, Everest's neighbor, with the great Khumbu Glacier icefall in the foreground.

was to learn the reason. "I lost all my toes from frost-bite," the Swiss told him. Then he added with a smile, "You hang on to yours."

Up and down, up and down through Nepal they went. At last they were so close to Everest that other mountains shut it from view. All they could see was the magic summit with its white plume of windblown snow. They made their base camp on Khumbu Glacier at 16,570 feet. And now the battle with the icefall began.

It was a terribly dangerous climb. Any moment towers of ice might come crashing down. Any moment someone might sink into a snow-hidden crevasse. They tried going this way and that. In a sheltered place halfway up the fall they managed to set up Camp Two. Then almost

Tenzing Norgay, Sherpa "Tiger."

at the top they came to what they knew they would find—the great crevasse. They must get across. Otherwise they might as well give up all hopes and dreams of the summit.

Back and forth along the edge of the crevasse they went, studying the mighty crack. It was much bigger than they had imagined it would be, and there seemed to be no way of solving the problem. Then someone offered a suggestion. Couldn't one of them swing across on a rope fastened to the rim?

Asper, the youngest of the party, at once offered to try. He tried again and again. He could swing across all right. But he couldn't catch hold of the smooth ice on the far side either with his fingers or with his ax. Each time he came back with a crash.

Suddenly one of the party pointed down in great excitement. "See! There is a shelf!" he cried.

They looked. And indeed, sixty feet down in the crevasse a sort of platform jutted out. A man might be able to cross over from it to the other wall. They put a rope around Asper and let him down. They held their breath while he crossed. Then, slowly, he chopped his way up. At the top he sank down exhausted. But he was on the other side, and now everything was all right. For now the rope could be made fast, other ropes could be thrown over, and they would soon have a bridge.

The hardest problem had become the easiest.

Day after day the Sherpas climbed the icefall with their packs. They crawled over the rope bridge. And there they were in the Valley of Silence.

During the next three weeks the Swiss set up camp after camp. They climbed part way up Lhotse, then veered to the left and brought goods halfway up to a point they called the saddle. It was at the base of Everest's east ridge. Now at last they were in a position to try for the saddle itself. If they got there, they would try for the top.

Tenzing had a double job now. He was still sirdar. It was still his business to see that the Sherpas got with their loads where they were supposed to. But now he had also been chosen to be one of the climbing team. He was a real member of the expedition. He and Lambert —whom he loved and respected above all other companions—were always on the same rope.

On the morning of May 27, 1952, Tenzing, Lambert, and two other mountaineers plodded across the saddle and started up the east ridge of Everest. They were the chosen climbers who would try for the top. At about 27,500 feet they stopped, for they had gone as far as they could that day. The plan was to dump the tent and the few supplies they had brought and come up again next day with more. But it was a beautiful day, and a daring idea took hold of Tenzing.

"Sahib," he said to Lambert, "we ought to stay here tonight—you and I."

Lambert smiled and their eyes met. He had been thinking the same thing. The fine weather was too rare to miss. He and Tenzing should make a try in the morning.

So that's how it was settled. The others went down, and the two friends pitched their tent. They had no sleeping bags. There was no stove. They ate a little cheese. Tenzing melted some snow over a candle, and they drank the snow water. Then they lay down on the tent floor. They didn't even try to sleep. All night long as they waited for dawn, they rubbed and slapped each other to keep from freezing. "Tomorrow—you and I," Tenzing kept saying.

In the gray morning they looked out—and their hearts sank. The weather had worsened. But at least it wasn't snowing. They could still make their try.

Their oxygen tanks were so heavy that before long they decided to drop them. But without oxygen they could move only at a snail's pace. First one would lead, then the other. Up, up, hour after hour—and every hour seeming a week long. Moving carefully because there was a precipice on one side and a cornice of snow jutting out over the other. Cutting steps. Barely creeping along.

Panting, gasping, taking three breaths for each step. And the weather getting worse all the time.

Now their bodies were bent double against the wind and driving snow, and they no longer thought about anything. They were machines that moved and stopped and moved again. Just to put one foot in front of the other demanded all they had. Another step, one more.

Then they stopped and didn't move again. Silently they looked up at the mountain. In five hours they had made 650 feet in height, and the south summit was still 500 feet above them. The *south* summit, not the *true* summit. That lay somewhere still higher up.

They didn't trust themselves to exchange a glance. Without a word, with one accord, they turned back. They knew that to go on would be to die. They might make the top. But they could never get back alive.

On the following day the second team could not get beyond the saddle. The members of the expedition dreamed now only of what they would do next time, what they would do differently when they came back in the fall.

In the fall they were on the mountain again. Once more, Tenzing and Lambert tried desperately. For it had become the hope of their lives that they would get to the top together. But this time the wind proved too strong. The cold was too fierce. They couldn't make it.

On top of the world

On the east ridge of Everest, 27,900 feet up, two men lay in a tent while gusts of wind tried to blow it away. They were members of a British expedition—33-year-old Edmund Hillary, a New Zealand beekeeper, and Tenzing, now 39. They dozed and woke, dozed and woke. Each time they woke, they listened. What would the weather be like in the morning when they made their try?

At about 3:30 A.M. Tenzing got the stove going. He boiled snow for lemon juice and coffee, and they ate a little food left over from their supper. Then they opened the tent flap and looked out. It was clear and quiet!

"May 29, 1953," Tenzing thought. "A year ago, almost to the day, Lambert and I came down in defeat." And in his heart he prayed, "God of my father and mother, be good to me today."

He had slept with his boots on. But Hillary had taken his off, and now they were frozen hard as iron. It was a bad start. Hillary was upset. Would his feet get frostbitten? More important, would he and Tenzing get to the top? If they made the summit, the expedition meant to present the victory as a coronation gift to young

As the 1953 expedition started out, each porter carried a 40-pound load.

Queen Elizabeth. Would they fail because he had taken off his boots?

For a whole hour the two men worked with the boots, heating them over the stove, pounding them, pulling them. At last they were soft enough to put on. Then the climbers got the rest of their things ready. They fastened their crampons to the soles of their boots. On their hands they put three pairs of gloves—silk, wool, and windproof. Tenzing carefully wound a red scarf round his neck. It was one that his good friend Lambert had given him, and he had been keeping it to wear on

this occasion. Swinging two oxygen bottles apiece on their backs, they went out.

Tenzing took the lead first. But they kept changing places on the rope in order to share the work of kicking and chopping footholds. They climbed well, for their oxygen tanks were of a new, improved kind. It wasn't long before Tenzing could point out the spot where Lambert and he had turned back on their heartbreaking try the previous spring. "How cold and windy it was then," the Sherpa remembered. "And now the sun is shining so brightly."

The south summit was not far ahead of them. But just before they reached it, they stopped to examine something that lay on the snow. It was two bottles of oxygen. Yesterday the first team had left the oxygen behind after failing to reach the top. "That's the way it is on a mountain," Tenzing thought gratefully. "Our comrades went down without oxygen so that Hillary and I might have more." They left the nearly full bottles for the trip down and turned to the ascent.

It had suddenly become much more difficult. They were going up a steep snow ridge. Every moment they feared they would be swept away, for they had almost no control. Yet somehow they kept their footing. Somehow they got by. And here they were on the south summit at the very place where yesterday's team had turned back. They looked up. They had only about 300 feet more to go.

But the ridge was narrower and steeper here. On their left the precipice fell away to the Valley of Silence 8,000 feet below. On their right, snow cornices jutted out over a 10,000-foot drop to the glacier. They would have to twist between precipice and cornices and watch every step. A few inches too far over to the left, a few inches too far to the right, and death would be waiting for them.

Just at this point, by good fortune, each came to the end of his first bottle of oxygen and could dump it. Luckily, too, beyond the south summit the snow was firm. Still, they didn't dare trust it, for if they got too far out on a cornice, it might break off. They took short steps, moving one at a time. And while one moved, the other fixed his ax in the snow for an anchor.

Higher, higher they climbed, picking their way carefully, balancing between death on one side and death on the other. They were on the lookout for a rock cliff which they had seen on photographs from the air. And here it was, standing directly in their path. Would they be able to get around it? Hillary, who was leading, explored.

Between the rock and the inner side of a snow cornice was a narrow gap. Could he squeeze his body through it? There was great danger, of course, that the cornice would break off. But he must try, for there was no other way. He pressed backward with his feet against the snow—and it held. He was all right. Tenzing, standing below, belayed him while Hillary worked his way up the gap. He pushed, pushed—and drew himself out on a platform above. Tenzing followed, Hillary pulling on the rope.

They knew that now the worst was over. They knew they were very near the top. They took a few good breaths of oxygen, then bent for the last effort.

There were cornices on both sides of them now, but the ridge was less steep. A lot of snowy humps ahead, one above the other. Then a long snow slope. . . .

Just a hundred more feet to go. They passed bare rocks, then more snow humps. And now the way was wide enough for two to go side by side, and the slope was easy. They were climbing, climbing still. But suddenly they didn't need to climb any more. They were on top, on the summit of Everest, on Chomolungma, on the Mountain-So-High-No-Bird-Can-Fly-Over-It.

They shook hands. But for Tenzing this wasn't nearly enough. He threw his arms around Hillary. They thumped each other on the back till they were almost out of breath. Then they turned off their oxygen and looked around. On every side of them were the great

Photograph of Tenzing taken by Hillary on the summit.

Himalayas—and every single peak was below them. They stood on the highest mountain of all.

"Never, never will I see a sight like this again," Tenzing thought. "Chomolungma is like a mother hen and the other mountains are chicks under her wings."

Hillary had taken out his camera. Tenzing unwound four little flags he had tied around his ax—the flags of the United Nations, of Great Britain, of Nepal, and of India. He held the ax up and Hillary took his picture.

Then, while Hillary took photographs of the mountains, Tenzing attended to a little ceremony of his own. Kneeling down, he scraped a hollow in the ice. In the hollow he laid a packet of candies and the stub of a red-and-blue pencil which his little daughter had given him. With a silent prayer, he covered up these offerings to Chomolungma.

"How many men have dreamed of standing on this spot!" he thought. "Hillary and I are the ones to do it, but we could never have done it without all those others who dreamed and tried and failed." Those others seemed very close. They seemed to be there on the mountain with them, and closest of all was Lambert.

Tenzing put up his hand to the red scarf and drew it tighter. A little bit of Lambert had got here anyhow, he thought.

Hillary came over. He had finished taking his pictures for the record and was ready to go. They turned on their oxygen for the long way down.

Tenzing and Hillary resting at a high camp on the day after their victorious climb.

Paiju in the Himalayas—a peak as yet unclimbed.

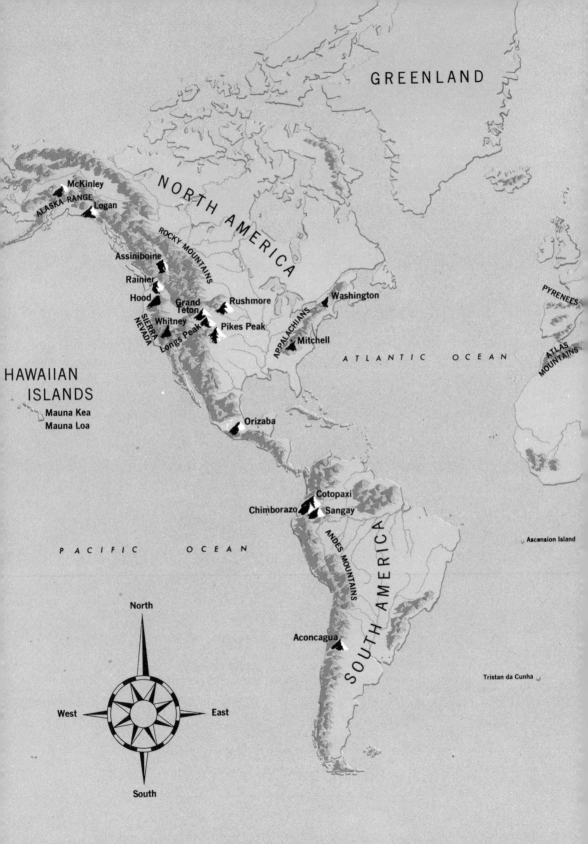

GREENLAND

NORTH AMERICA

McKinley

ALASKA RANGE

Logan

ROCKY MOUNTAINS

Assiniboine

Rainier

Hood

SIERRA NEVADA

Whitney

Grand Teton

Longs Peak

Rushmore

Pikes Peak

Washington

APPALACHIANS

Mitchell

HAWAIIAN ISLANDS

Mauna Kea
Mauna Loa

ATLANTIC OCEAN

PYRENEES

ATLAS MOUNTAINS

Orizaba

PACIFIC OCEAN

Cotopaxi

Chimborazo

Sangay

Ascension Island

ANDES MOUNTAINS

SOUTH AMERICA

Aconcagua

Tristan da Cunha

North

West

East

South

Gall's Stereographic Projection, with two parallels at 45° N. and S. latitude

ARCTIC OCEAN

URALS

EUROPE

ASIA

ALPS
Matterhorn
Mont Blanc
Vesuvius
Olympus

CAUCASUS
Elbrus

K2 (Godwin-Austen)

HIMALAYAS

Everest

Kangchenjunga

INDIA

JAPAN
Fuji

PACIFIC

OCEAN

AFRICA

Kenya
Kilimanjaro

INDIAN OCEAN

AUSTRALIA

NEW
ZEALAND

Table Mountain

Cook

SOME IMPORTANT MOUNTAINS
OF THE WORLD

Liam Dunne

INDEX